Shine Bright:
Inside out like a Candle!

Author

R.Z. Joseph

Copyright © 2013 Shine Bright Inside Out like a Candle.

New Dreams, Colors and Faces.

All rights reserved. Revised 2nd Edition/Ages 16 up.

ISBN:0991156315
ISBN-13:978-0-9911563-1-3

DEDICATION

S. L. Johnson
For your steadfast love and support.

Vicky, Chermaine & Robert Black
For helping me launch my dream!

To
My parents
Alfred and Agnes
And
Siblings

Loving Memories
Marie-Therese R. Joseph
Grandma Mom
RIP

Verona Charles
Granny Iya
RIP

Ma James
RIP

INTRODUCTION

If you need motivation to pick yourself up- after life has given you its own doses of double kicks – this book is for you!

Get up! A new day has come for you to Shine Bright!

You can recover by knowing who sent you here and why!

Find out your real Self-Worth as a favored child of God!

I know each crisis carries a seed for a better opportunity! Find yours within these pages!

Shine Bright is an unconventional path to Self-Esteem and Self-Reliance to live your best life!

Go for whatever your creator has told you to pursue- a loving family, clothes, cars, house, land, money and the power to get wealth!

How can you give to charity if you are broke?

Claim prosperity for yourself and become what you envision!

You are a winner! Believe, take action and you will have it!

Shine Bright- inside out like a candle! My gift to you. God Bless.

With Goodwill,

R. Z. Joseph

TABLE OF CONTENTS

1. Unveiling
2. Recognition
3. Values
4. Different
5. Born
6. Beliefs
7. Revelation
8. Seek
9. Proof
10. Unique
11. Identity
12. Mind-Spirit
13. Citizen
14. Son
15. Male
16. Daughter
17. Girls
18. Woman
19. Female
20. Names
21. Invisible
22. Faith
23. Visible
24. Story-Tellers
25. Profilers
26. Wise-Men
27. Awakening
28. Kingdom
29. Self-Awareness
30. Senses
31. Characteristics
32. Nationality

33. Rights
34. Being
35. Beliefs
36. Process
37. Original Blue Prints
38. Beginning
39. Recap
40. Action
41. Contemplation
42. Self- Love
43. Excavation
44. Chiseling
45. Rebirth
46. Vision
47. Focus
48. Work
49. Service
50. Candle/me
51. Questions
52. Light
53. Assurance
54. Examples
55. Clarity
56. Death
57. Darkness
58. Mirror
59. Fail, then Succeed
60. Success
61. Here to Serve
62. The Call

"The Mind once enlightened, **cannot** again become dark"

Thomas Paine

CHAPTER 1 UNVEILING

Born in a family,
Nurtured with help from
Doctors, nurses, teachers, pastors or Priests
And the list goes on.

Birth Certificate,
Vaccinations,
First Communion,
Adult Baptism,
Rites of passage,
Identification cards,
Family albums,
School pictures,
All reminders of me.

Born rich or poor,
To a loving family or
One of conflicts,
Nurtured or tolerated-
Loved by the community or a
Social outcast-
I exist!

I know I exist,
My Creator knows I live,
I am alive for a reason!

CHAPTER 2 RECOGNITION

I am created in my
Creator's likeness and image.
I am a small expression of
The big Creator called:
I AM
The ONE GOD.

I may be any gender but
I was born free!
I am a physical,
Hopeful spirit, trying to connect with others.

Connecting through my
Exquisite mind,
Social Media,
Schools,
Clubs,
Church,
Books,
New Technology,
Fashion and Fads.

I master behaviors
And habits,
From good or bad sources in my society.
I am a social being!

CHAPTER 3 VALUES

I learn
Children and women must be seen
And not heard-
An unfair rule if meant to stifle the aspirations
Of females and children on the globe.

I know
Free countries with democratic constitutions,
Decree rights and justice for both the young and aged.

I respect
Equal rights for males and females,
Including children too- boys and girls.

I hope
Communism and sponsored Terrorism states
Will have democracy without excessive greed,
Like the United States of America.
I have a right to be free!

CHAPTER 4 DIFFERENT

I know the struggles of:
Being different because of my
Race,
Gender,
Religion,
Politics,
Age,
Sexual Preference,
Social Class or Status,
And Nationality.

I seek to unveil
Things beneath my skin to
Understand the reasons
Why am I created in this physical body?

I wonder,
"Am I born to play role reversal games- example
Once a man, twice a child?"
I am different for a reason!

CHAPTER 5 BORN

Why was I given life?
To be the pawn of a religious fanatic?
Or
Fascist Politician?
Or
A bait for terrorist activities?
Or
An experiment in a laboratory?
Or
Is it to create my own life through trials and errors?
Or
Am I a reincarnation of my previous life?

I look in my mirror and I see me
Staring at three features in one face-
Parents,
Race,
And I see me- enclosed in flesh!

Who am I?
Why am I here on earth in this century at this moment in time?
Where do I begin?

R. Z. Joseph

CHAPTER 6 BELIEFS

As a child,
I believed
Whatever I was told by my society's story tellers:
Religion,
Sociology,
Psychology,
History,
Cultures,
Family,
Politics,
Television,
Friends,
Information Technology
And enemies- those closest to me, fronting as friends!

I had fears of lack
And a need to fill a deep empty hole within my heart-
Caused by childhood lies or abuses.

I had fears of Heaven and of Hell.
I hated darkness and talk of evil or death,
And church was more "Do as I say, not as I do".

But as a child,
I always believed in a Good GOD!

SHINE BRIGHT: INSIDE OUT, LIKE A CANDLE!

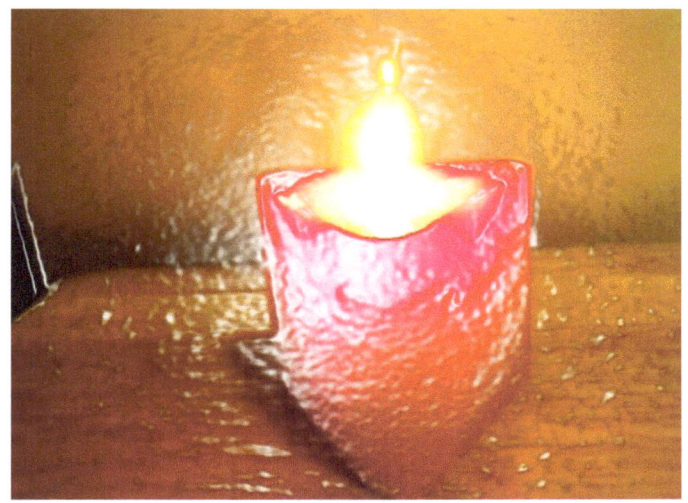

CHAPTER 7 REVELATION

The WORD of TRUTH
Entered my mind
And excavated doubts!

I blossomed into petals of
Awakening,
Like an unfolding Rose- the Rose of Sharon!

The WORD talked of REDEMPTION for
Past failures, wrong thinking, hurts
And
Misunderstandings.

Unlike some of those misguided
Storytellers who'd labeled me:
"Lost, unloved, addict, loser, outcast"

WORD said
"The TRUTH shall make you free!"

What TRUTH?

The truth of my existence!

CHAPTER 8 SEEK

The Creator,
In telepathic thoughts told me
"You are my original design,
An awaken mind, heart and spirit-
The most revered blue print on earth called Human Genome!"

I wanted to believe HIS Telepathy,
But needed proof on earth to validate HIS words.

I found out
A blue print of my human features was completed
In April 2003 for the first time in History –
And that Story Teller didn't lie!

God was proven right!
I am an original design of awaken Mind
And everything else that exist between
The Big I AM and the little I am- Me!

CHAPTER 9 PROOF

I can be read by Forensics – a TRUTH story teller!

My body is made up of chemicals whose interactions,
Are regulated by my Genetic Blue Print or DNA matter-
Drawn at the moment of my birth and yours –
False Psychics beware!

No two persons--except for twins, share the same DNA
matter
Or
Genes
Or
Chromosomes.

DNA matter determines my
Race,
Skin,
Blood,
Semen or Cum,
Saliva,
Hair or Color types and textures.

Forensic experts can prove anyone's
Genetic makeup and its differences with
Recognition software for my
Face,
Eyes,
Voice,
Teeth,
And even finger prints - so criminals beware!

CHAPTER 10 UNIQUE

Zero, point, zero one percent of DNA matter-
Written **0.01%** DNA, is <u>*NOT*</u> shared.
It is different in each individual!
I am a unique person!
GOD made no clones – try again you patent forgers!

Ninety-nine, point, ninety-nine percent DNA matter-
Expressed as 99.99% DNA is **SHARED**.
And is common to all people, whatever our race!

My humanity is common to all people- whatever their skin color:
2 hands,
2 ears,
2 feet,
1 mouth,
1 nose,
10 fingers and 10 toes!

Blood can be transfused
Or
Organs can be transplanted:
Kidneys, liver, eyes
And the list goes on.

I repeat:
DNA determines our humanity:
Body parts with a slight difference of 0.01 percent!

I am Unique for a reason – Red or Yellow, Black or White!

CHAPTER 11 MIND-SPIRIT

I can be seen.
I can be felt.
And seemingly operate
As an invisible person in
A visible, physical body!

I become--
Whatever the title or label of
The role I choose to play:
Child,
Student,
Mother,
Father,
Foster Parent,
Teacher,
Policeman,
Husband,
Wife,
Army veteran,
Nurse,
Poet,
Preacher,
Artist,
Writer,
Novice or
Master.

Positive or negative roles –

I am mind over matter
Or
Matter over mind – one and the same!

SHINE BRIGHT: INSIDE OUT, LIKE A CANDLE!

CHAPTER 12 IDENTITY

Today I know a little more about myself.

I am a gender,
I am somebody's child,
I belong to a race.
I have a distinct, genetic type or DNA sequence.

I am a different, individual with a personality.
I am one unique person among seven billion persons on the planet!
I repeat:
I am 1 of 7 billion unique persons on the six continents!

My DNA formula is 3 billion letters long-
Almost half the population of the entire, global earth!
It would take 5000 paperback books to print my genetic code!
Or
300 boxes of A4-Letter size paper
To store my genetic information,
Or
Storage on several compressed files on CDs or USB drives!

My spit on a gene testing chip or strip
Can tell you in a few hours-
More about me
Than I can say about me or you in 24 hours!

I am not a carbon copy-neither are you!

CHAPTER 13 CITIZEN

I am a Global Citizen in a Global Village – 21St century style! With the right skills, information and attitude I hope to excel.

I can express myself in tangible ways—
Mama,
Papa,
Professor,
Software Designer,
Fashion Model,
Hip Hop Artist,
Basketball player,
Pop Star,
Builder,
Singer,
Pianist,
Priest,
Rabbi,
Muslim,
Jew,
Christian,
Buddhist,
Chef,
Baker—
I am whatever title I decide.

I choose to become self-reliant!

CHAPTER 14 SON

Different from a girl,
Born a boy with a distinct body type and stride,
With an urgent need to be fed, clothed and loved.

First, by mommy dearest- protector, nurturer,
Maybe a bit too possessive to daughter-in-law-
The real wife-yes!

A grown male with rippling muscles
Or
A soft, jelly-like pot belly – dude go exercise!
Born to be cherished by girls with crushes
Or
Ladies with loud, thumping heart beats.

A hunter by nature,
Maybe with a virile appetite,
One who chases to his heart's content,
Until he settles down—I hope.

I am a son!

CHAPTER 15 MALE

Lover, provider, husband,
Life partner, Prince, President,
King, Chief Executive Officer or Dad- his roles!

The heart beat is the same for those he love
With his need to be loved and adored.

A heart with different feelings or expressions:
A hug
Or
A peck on a cheek--- a pat on the back,
Or
A fervent kiss for his lover
Or
A command for
"Time out, you naughty child!"

Satisfied with challenges:
Sports, career, competition, food and sexual exploits!

Christianity advocates sons or males
To marry women or females,
Some choose alternatives – other males.

A son whatever his life preference
Is
The pride of his family, friends and community!

I am a male – gay or straight, I exist!

R. Z. Joseph

CHAPTER 16 DAUGHTER

What pulsating, sated joy to be a dear daughter!

The idea of moms or dads dressing her--
In pink frills and yards of ribbons of all shades of color!

First, she's a dream come true for parents!
The appearance of shiny hair with a triumphant scream at birth-
Gave parents the gift of nurturing a dear, daughter – I know!

A daughter, moody or finicky like her mom or dad.
Adopted or naturally birthed or a foster child,
The love for her is still the same-binding!

Born to be curvaceous, she is disgusted by pimples and bad hair days!

I am a dear daughter, too!

CHAPTER 17 GIRLS

Born with natural locks, wavy or straight,
A girl loves to style her hair- whether natural or store bought!

A girl—the debutante or social butterfly,
Smart, educated, witty, fashion conscious---
Always sweet smelling, spending loads of money
On brand name perfumes, shoes, purses and dresses!
Let's hope she has a job to support her splurges—yes!

A daughter-one day Prom Queen,
Next day cheer Leader or the Star at her wedding
Or baby shower – single or wedded, she is adored!

A lady - at Sorority or Board Meetings she is so much fun,
To bank your money on-literally!

I am a girl – high five!!!

CHAPTER 18 WOMAN

Born to be mother or wife—
Lawyer,
Secretary of State,
Prime Minister,
First Lady,
Princess,
Chief Executive Officer,
Governor,
Senator
Or
United States President—
Hilary 2016, would be nice!
She would aim for the stars
To shatter glass ceilings-like Michelle Obama!

A woman shines like a bright candle!
No less than a son or male or boy,
Yet an aura of special beauty, ignited by GOD,
To make life on earth complete!

She turns grown men
Into little boys who fight to be noticed
They race to be her first to:
Friend, date or marry.

I am a woman –yes!

CHAPTER 19 FEMALE

Some places allow for marriage between females
Despite our traditional way of having female and male
partners.

The Globe is not about me and my beliefs—alone.
The world is made up of many people with beliefs—
Some similar.

Our Global Village has 7 billion people of several
Different:
Races,
Tribes,
Kingdoms,
Politics,
Religion,
History,
Beliefs and
Moods!

I have to respect
The legal rights of others
According to the laws of my society, country or state.

Females have rights to other life styles
And discrimination or homophobia
Against Lesbians or Gay men,
Is a Crime punishable in most courts of law on the Globe!
Let wisdom, conscience and laws guide me,
Secular or Spiritual Laws? Both.

I have a right to choose my life partner!

R. Z. Joseph

© 2013 All Rights Reserved. New Dreams, Colors and Faces.

CHAPTER 20 NAMES

Some call me woman, man or brother or sister.
Or
Names I use out in the open or in my closet.

Some call me Black or White,
Latino or Spanish,
East Indian or American Indian,
British citizen or West Indian.

To be honest,
I dislike names like
African-Americans.
I was happy when
Comedienne Goldberg, replied
"Why not American!"

Can I find the real me in such names?
No!

I am a whole person,
I look in my mirror—
I see me stare back at me!
Therefore, recognize me and---
Say my name correctly!
Repeat after me:

Your name

CHAPTER 21 INVISIBLE

I am a feeling entity at the very core of my inner being!
At least that is how I feel!

I am a thinking person,
That is what my thoughts in my mind tell me.

I am different from you by
How I do or say the same thing
You are thinking to express or sort out.
Our arrangement of words and actions are suited to each:
Original, like lines under my feet or in our hands
And inner cheeks inside our mouths!

I matter to my family or those who support me
Or
Others who help maintain my well-being for the right reasons!

I am Special that is what the thoughts in my mind and heart tell me.

The real me---
Feels invisible, hidden from sight when I talk to you!
The real you,
Feel the same way as you react to what you are reading!
Where are we really connecting?

I am a feeling, invisible entity connecting with others!

CHAPTER 22 FAITH

Theologians or Bible preachers say
I was born with good virtues
Before my Original Blue Print for Good was hijacked
With sinful viruses or vices by fallen angels or hijackers.

Philosophers differ in how they view my life,
Atheists said "No God, you are on your own!"
Agnostics replied" Maybe!"

My philosophy is scientist proved what my Bible first said:
"You are wonderfully made!" and
"Faith is what you believe is true till you see it!"

I cannot depend on what people tell me about me-
I have to depend on things that make sense in the WORD!
And, Shine like a Candle- inside and out!

I am a believer!

CHAPTER 23 VISIBLE

I am a Complex, complicated, human being.
I am made up of many inside connections:
Bones,
Energy-spirit vibes,
Cartilage,
Flesh,
Hormones or fluids,
Gastric juices,
Bile,
Muscles and much Biology.

I am an intricate, combination system of physical parts-
Some you see and others inside with invisible hook-ups—
Like live wires, with the power to hurt or heal!

I am made up of 23 pairs of Chromosomes or DNA substance:
A total of 46 – twenty-three from my mama and papa each.
Look at me under a magnifying, microscopic or x-ray instruments,
See some of what goes on in your body- ask a few story tellers:
EKG readers, Forensic experts, Airport scanners or the FBI
– ask!

I am a person in a physical body having different experiences!

SHINE BRIGHT: INSIDE OUT, LIKE A CANDLE!

R. Z. Joseph

SHINE BRIGHT: INSIDE OUT, LIKE A CANDLE!

CHAPTER 24 STORY-TELLERS

Some say I have no divinity,
A Psalmist called me god- I am of I AM?

Christians say God's Holy Spirit lives in my body—
If I believe in JESUS CHRIST.

Prophets and Philosophers imply:
My life is spiritually hidden and covered--
By huge, wide webs of spiritual and legal laws.

I am protected by spiritual laws:
'Above and below'.
To protect my mind and body to enjoy:
Inner peace, balance and pursuit of happiness!

A lie exist that:
I was born a tiny cell who evolved into a hunched back ape!
And then in time
I became an upright, walking human with good manners.

I am not an ape—slave or free, I am human!
Attempts are made to clone animals and food
These may be good
To cure diseases and feed our poor
But I am not a clone!
Am I aware of the ethics of cloning humans?
Is it possible to clone the spirit inside a fake body?

I am an Original Human Being and my name is
_____

(Your Name)

CHAPTER 25 PROFILERS

Sociologists infer my mind is shaped by centuries of information,
And habits passed on from generations of my ancestors and society.

Anthropologists suggest my peculiar likes or dislikes for certain foods,
And jobs or crafts are rooted in cultures past from Communal blood lines.

Psychologists construct tests to diagnose my personality,
And mind, to tell me which tasks in life I am more suited for---
They predict with accuracy my mental suitability for certain jobs.

All those profilers are right to some extent,
But---
I and only I,
Can express the real me!

I can think for myself!

CHAPTER 26 WISE-MEN

Wise men say I am part of a magnetic, energetic field--
Connecting all of us in the entire sphere of existence- dead or alive!

Some say through life's trials,
I learn my karmic lessons:
Right from wrong—
Good from bad.

Others say I was born male or female
With the same rights in God's sight!
And, children and adults all share basic rights--
Sanctioned by the United Nations too!

I believe that Sin and Evil exist in certain realms,
But have no place in GOD's space,
Where only GOOD dwells.

I am a child of God, born for a purpose!

R. Z. Joseph

CHAPTER 27 AWAKENING

An inner knowing,
As if beamed into my inner mind
By a million volts of fast, loud thoughts!

I am a Human Being!
Possibly GOD's greatest masterpiece in the earth!

Duplicated by new technologies to imitate my human qualities:
Movement,
Language,
Speech,
Artificial Intelligence,
(Thinking?)
Writing,
Playing,
Running,
The list is endless, but we know real from fake!

My Creator calls me:
"A Holy, Body Temple!"

I am a Conscious being!

CHAPTER 28 KINGDOM

I believe I am a Creative being.
Look at my life- whether good or bad,
I created certain situations in my life,
And I can change what I don't like!

I can create good consequences
With right thinking and right actions.
Knowing I am a Creative being,
Who can feel and think, makes me feel loved!

The WORD says:
"God's Kingdom is within me"
Interpretation:
The creative process for anything
Begins inside your mind!
In your thoughts—good or bad.

I am aware of my good thoughts in my mind!

CHAPTER 29 AWARENESS

I am aware of my real identity!
Like a satellite with endless effects
That is connected to cell phones,
Or other wireless technology:
I can be felt in spirit or soul or mind!

Look at me, my:
Head,
Color of my skin,
Height,
Weight—90 or 900 pounds—
I love all of me!

My body rocks—
My nose, hips, eyes, toes, derriere,
Male or female:
Blind, deaf, dumb,
Crooked or straight—
Disabled or old,
I love me from head to toe!

Age brings wisdom and grey hairs,
Maybe loss of teeth or limb-
I will always feel good about me!

Young or old I can dance—check my moves!
Mama, Grandpa, Great Grand, Auntie or Uncle:
I feel like a Grand Marshall or Belle of the Ball-Proud!

I am like an unseen, electrical current that can be felt.
Though unseen by the naked, physical eyes,
I can express myself through thoughts and actions.

I am light in darkness, starlight if you please!

R. Z. Joseph

CHAPTER 30 SENSES

My intuitive, discerning mind is alive- like a scanner!
Though invisible or unseen,
I'm a powerful force for good or ill,
I am like a light that ignores the darkness!

I decide my path whenever I choose—whatever my moods:
Happy, confused, sad or depressed- results happen.

I am guided by wisdom:
Right information for clear thinking,
To harvest an abundance of positive actions—
With good consequences for myself and others!

Who more am I?
I am one of a kind—no one like me on earth or in the Heavens!
No boast, just the forensic facts!
What's my evidence?
Remember my DNA report? The 0.01 percent!

I have intuition- I sense without my two eyes!
I am like the scanner in a printer-
Checking situations, people and places,
To know who is for me or against me,
For my protection and peace of mind.

R. Z. Joseph

CHAPTER 31 CHARACTERISTICS

I live among seven billion other custom made designer originals,
I currently live in North America, while you live
_____,
I reside on one of our six continents or somewhere in the Galaxies as
A NASA Astronaut or Russian Explorer or Spy – for good, not ill.

I am alive and well in a Global Village of diverse cultures,
And people with different world views.

I make contact via intricate networks of emotions or activities:
Thoughts,
Desires,
Actions,
Business- profits or losses,
Partnerships or mergers-
Like a marriage or divorce:
Temporary or permanent!

I am aware of my place in the world!

CHAPTER 32 NATIONALITY

Some call me Asian from the continent of Asia:
I may be Chinese
Or
East Indian from India – a Hindu worshipper
Or
A Punjabi from Pakistan – maybe a Muslim who studies the Koran.

I may live on the continent of South or North America
Or Europe
Or Africa – a Nigerian or Moroccan,
Or Antarctica,
Or I may live on the Arctic Circle – as an Eskimo.

But I feel like the Equator!
I am:
An invisible line,
Which circles the Globe of Human Experience –
As a baby, young child, adult, senior citizen – sinner or saint!

What is my fate on earth or after I die—do I truly die?
Hell or Heaven?
Resurrection?
Rapture?
Reincarnation?

A trip like Biblical Elijah in a chariot of fire.
He shined so bright from the inside out like a candle!

I am a national of _____

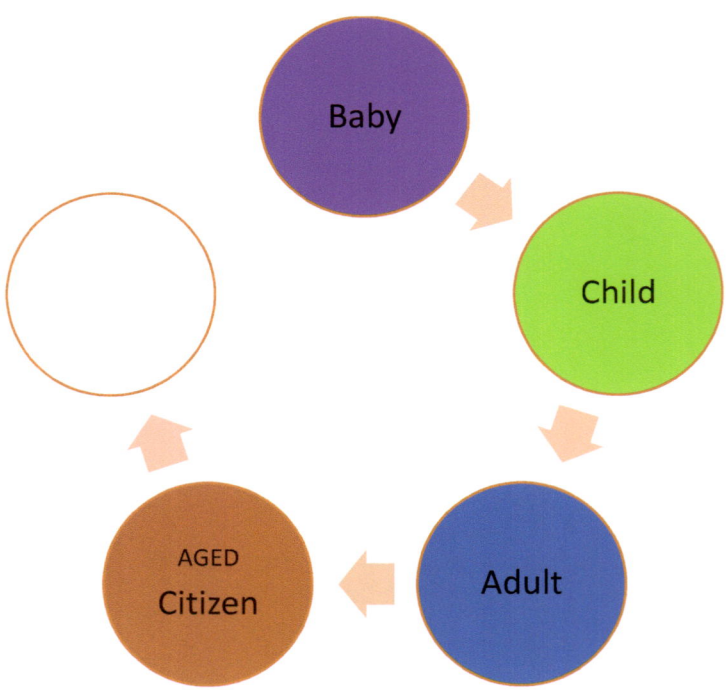

CHAPTER 33 RIGHTS

I am a spirit-body with spiritual access to Heavens' throne room through prayer and fasting --if I am a believer.

I am a Human being with legal rights on earth, in our Global Village — Believer or non-believer!

I was born free like the first man and woman in the Garden of Eden-

Or whatever the Koran or Torah or my religious beliefs espouse!

I have rights!

Yet some people may violate the basic ones:
Access to education,
Fair elections,
Work- with equal pay for men and women!
Free speech and even to have a family or a home!

Children, women and men all have rights, including:
Not to be abused or molested,
Or forced into child labor or slavery!

If anyone tries to abuse me, I will not keep silent!
I will complain to those in authority:
Parents, Teachers, Social workers, Policemen and lawyers.

I know my rights at home and in public- so back off bully!

R. Z. Joseph

CHAPTER 34 BEING

Some people keep dividing me into:
Third World, Advance Society or Developing State –
Based on my country's 20th century economy—
News flash:
The economy has gone Global in the 21st Century!

Whatever my geographic location-Bangkok or New York:
I am a citizen in the Galaxies, like a dot in a liquid sea of
Creative specks, of sparkling human and spirit activities!

I feel like a free, spirit camouflage in a physical body—
Having a soul or spirit experience with others on earth and
in The Heavens!

I feel I can fly, wherever I choose to go,
With my inner mind of imaginative vision,
And connective access to GOD's Omniscient mind-
All Knowing or Universal.

I feel like a flame on a wick, enclosed in a candle!

CHAPTER 35 BELIEFS

I believe:
I am a Child of
The Omnipresent GOD- who is everywhere!

I believe
I was first an idea in GOD's Mind,
Until my biological parents requested me—
With thoughts and an action of love or lust.
It doesn't matter how I arrive on the Globe-
I am happy to be here!

I believe in:
One GOD,
One LOVE,
One FAITH,
GOOD WORKS—
In earth and Heavenly dimensions.

I believe
GOD"S TRUE CHURCH
Includes people from all nationalities on the Globe:
Sorry False prophets and doom-Sayers, NOT!

I am GOD's helping hands!

CHAPTER 36 PROCESS

I look at myself in a mirror,
I first connect with the real me in spirit form-
Looking at the physical me with my soul's eye!
Which some call a Third or Discerning eye.

Perfection of spirit or soul matter:
I see no flaws, no color or race,
I see the real me!

I see many explicable and inexplicable things at once!
Suffice to say, I sense more than I see!

An image full of senses:
Smell, Sight, Touch, Taste, Sound!
The sixth sense,
And much more.

I appear to others as a face with a racial identity,
Yet to my Creator I stand like Eve or Adam stood-
A replica of GOD- created in his likeness and image!

The Biblical Psalmist called me god- I am of I AM?

CHAPTER 37 ORIGINAL BLUE PRINTS

Adam and Eve, first humans.
I pine for all their free stuff:
A peaceful setting,
Food on trees,
Right atmospheric or body temperature,
Clean water to drink and bathe-
Freedom to roam naked, in total privacy!

Today, to have these things,
I have to get money to pay for:
An education,
Study,
Get skilled,
Graduate,
And work hard for a fraction of all they had!

By the way who was Adam's mother?
Some people call the Earth: Mother Earth.
Was GOD both Mama and Papa to Adam?

Bible says Adam gave his rib to form Eve.
Did that make her a clone? No!
GOD breathed life into them both
And they became Original Conscious Beings!

Ah, but this is not about Adam, Science or Religion,
It's about my existence – who am I and why am I here?
I exist, the Creator knows I live, I am alive for a reason!

CHAPTER 38 BEGINNING

There is a wise saying,
"You need to go back to the very beginning,
To understand yourself".

Which beginning?

The time of my conception in God's mind?
Or
The time my biological parents engaged in sex to birth me?
Or
When I showed up in America from Cambodia with my
adoptive parents?
Or
A drug addict popping, puffing, snorting or injecting drugs?
Or
Acting the fool- lying, cheating, stealing and reckless?

Beginnings are all the same:
It's the discovery of self!

Who am I?
Naked or Clothed,
Or
Veiled and disguised,
Beneath flesh—
Permit me to de flesh!

I am in spirit form having a human experience in a body!

CHAPTER 39 RECAP

Today, I know more about myself.
I am a gender,
I am a child of God,
I am part of the big I AM,
I am dual- visible and invisible, whatever title or role
I choose to play!

I am a Global Citizen in the Global Village and entire Galaxies!
I am guided by laws- spiritual, legal or secular
For the Greater Good.

I have skills I can express in tangible or seen and
Intangible or unseen ways.

I am responsible for my life!

I have made a decision to be productive!

I will focus on my life.

CHAPTER 40 ACTION

Today, I will buy a journal and start listing my qualities, goals and vision.
And use my skills to better myself and others

I will honor my body temple,
I will eat healthy,
I will find out my Body Mass Index-
My special number to know my ideal weight and height for my age.

I will honor GOD by my choices of people, situations and career—
For my integrity and wholeness.
I will be duty bound to know my Life Expectancy Rate-
That special number predicting my years on earth:
Based on my family's history for taking care of needs-
To make me healthy, wealthy and wise.
And know that I have an expiry date in this life—
Before the next!

I am prepared to live my best life on earth
And honor GOD who covers me from HIS turf!
I am a child of a GOOD GOD!

SHINE BRIGHT: INSIDE OUT, LIKE A CANDLE!

CHAPTER 41 CONTEMPLATION

How long can I live in my physical body?
Am I literate according to 21st century standards?

Do I have computer skills to use the new devices that are replacing my old ways of reading, writing, spelling and communicating?

Am I equip with the right information, skills and resources?
Do I have Health or Life insurance or retirement earnings?
How long can I work based on my current age?
If I am sick-God forbids, who would take care of me?

Do I have a support system of people to care for me?
Do I have any money or assets to help me pay for my bills?
What forms of wealth or riches do I have – lands, houses, money or other valuables- like gold, stocks or bonds?

Do I have more assets than liabilities – debts I owe to business places or people or the government?
I hope I don't owe de tax man!
Do I have Wills– a Living Will too?
How would I like to be remembered?
I was born to figure out my life and win!

CHAPTER 42 SELF-LOVE

I appeared dressed to the world of sight,
And stood unveiled in front of my mirror,
Completely naked, de fleshed!

A mirror of my own choosing:
A fall from grace, my heart,
Water, Glass
Or
The Inner Mind---
I heard the sounds of jeers-mockers, but I grew deaf,
I accessed the Kingdom within and surrendered!

I loved all what and who I saw—
Curves, shapes, sounds, information and everything else
that lay:
As in Heaven, so on earth.

I saw prints of UNIVERSAL LOVE:
Stuck on fingers, hair, skin and toes!
Interlaced within bones and flesh,
I sensed carefree me in spirit form!
You sensed yourself too- de fleshed?

Connected to vital life forces- spheres of GOD or I AM,
As seen by Biblical Moses and Gideon,
As they too stood unveiled of manmade garbs--de fleshed,
Like Adam and Eve,
To answer Destiny's call!

I am unveiled, I am lit, see me Shine- inside out!

CHAPTER 43 EXCAVATION

I looked within and saw the Kingdom of GOD as told by
THE MASTER,
Everything he said was true, based on his measuring rod:
As above, so below.

Any need for sectarian beliefs—gone!
Sorry false teachers –NOT!

Only I mattered to understand myself,
To seek and be found by GOD who'd said,
"I will have no man teach you- I am found of them who seek me"

Future held at bay,
Until needed when the present was right!
Then I'd shape time to do my bidding,
As the rest remained—uncarved,
A block of candlewax, not needing a shape, model or a mold!

Any sign of cosmetics, a disability or age- out of sight!
No weave, toupee or prosthetics—all gone!
I stood de fleshed,
Behind The Veil in pure, spirit matter:
Present to self,
Absent to jeers!

I have GOD's Holy Spirit living inside me!

CHAPTER 44 CHISELING

My unveiling was necessary,
To see myself as GOD saw me!
To unwind my wounded soul of forced, societal roles!
Displayed on life's illusionary stage,
Which hid TRUTHS meant to set me free!

As I stood in front of my mirror,
All societal titles, right notes and missteps,
Those sessions, long over—gone!
I was drenched in a mood, for a Chivalric, spiritual ecstasy—alone!

My sacred mood required tossing names and faces aside- temporarily:
To make room for my creative self,
My innermost thoughts and aspirations!

A fire within me rose in a vibratory roar and something magical took over,
As mirror and mind faded into a divine partnership of sorts---
Like Daniel's in the Lion's Den, when GOD shut that Lion's mouth!
Or
Joseph in prison with his personal dream while interpreting other people's dreams!
I accessed that inner Kingdom,
And saw myself, as God sees me – Strong!

I am a Creative person – like you!

CHAPTER 45 REBIRTH

I felt a fresh spark with my own rhythmic, signature cycles and DNA intact!

I heard a heavenly choir of Angels sang a song in celebration,

As I entered the gateway to join those who had made the journey before:

The Redeemed? Biblical Moses stood front and center—yes?

What did the Christian Transfiguration prove?

That Moses had resurrected or Transition while in that unmarked grave? And Elijah had never died- was still alive, never tasting death or a resurrection? Through a mirror of GOD's own choosing, behind a symbolic veil?

Answer me MASTER! What about the three witnesses at the Transfiguration –Peter, James and John? Why three participants in the Transfiguration- JESUS, Moses and Elijah? Why the Trinity- FATHER, SON AND HOLY SPIRIT?

Why was the information passed on in my Holy Book?

Today, I will luxuriate in my triangular personality:

Me, Myself and I.

I love how I look- fat, thin, old, young, rich or poor,

I am, that I am? Creative being of the Original Creator?

SHINE BRIGHT: INSIDE OUT, LIKE A CANDLE!

CHAPTER 46 VISION

In my mirror,

I merged with other sparks in a sea of faces,

I saw many teachers, mentors, guides and player-haters-watching.

The detractors, I kept in my peripheral view,

As a mirage of Judas-conspirators, took shape,

I chose instead to be a harbinger of the GREATER GOOD.

As if on cue, from the image in my mirror, the soldier in me was set ablaze,

And I with steel-will seized my share of the Vision within.

I became a vessel, bearing child-like faith,

And saw more space within my vision,

To possess my place within the KINGDOM.

I was free to create without judging you or you judging me,

Because creative impressions were soul's undoing to show my real core – and yours: we got skills!

I need Vision to see my skills!

SHINE BRIGHT: INSIDE OUT, LIKE A CANDLE!

CHAPTER 47 FOCUS

My eyes are on the ultimate prize,

A secret stone, with my other name-

As told by the Biblical Revelator.

To live or die, both paths to awakening?

Displaying love or hate.

Pleasure or pain.

Why must a seed die to grow- and then bear fruit? Or branches pruned to bear more fruit?

Is pain a karmic reaction when I strayed from the right path ordained for me?

Ordained or pre destined? By whom?

Why?

When?

How?

Where?

What is involved?

My mind awoke with wisdom.

SHINE BRIGHT: INSIDE OUT, LIKE A CANDLE!

As I gazed at the naked glow

Of awakened, care-free me in the mirror of mind!

Created in the likeness of my Creator? Moses reported:

"I AM, that I am "

My mantra bears repetition:

My genetic makeup of 0.01 percent is unique!

Light reflects light!

I will shine bright as a candle flame!

CHAPTER 48 WORK

A call to service, mode of operation, customized to fit skills set.

My own, unique, signature style for creating whatever my GOD assigns—

On life's empty canvas to reflect my creativity, in whatever field I choose.

I give birth to the genius within—like you,

To create as Master from Omniscient or Universal Mind:

A place where interpretation is as intimate as our genetic blue prints!

Worlds and dimensions influx in space,

Attune each mind to one's authentic place—

Through events on life's canvas-

As each painted his own interpretation of GOD in the mirror of MIND.

SHINE BRIGHT: INSIDE OUT, LIKE A CANDLE!

Among those artists each exist in spirit in the:

Beginning,

Present and future –

Like a world, without an end!

I enjoy my work, which keeps me productive.

CHAPTER 49 SERVICE

My swift, loud strokes heard on life's canvas were emissions of my notes.

Echoes in the symphony of other geniuses.

Authentic above the noise of shadows—haters, fear, false beliefs, big egos and impure intentions – evil.

As my skills set took over,

Imagination and guts were gifts given to shape into the visible:

Things that were real or illusions.

I painted as unveiled mentors assisted-

With Servers, as they gathered as if by mystical hints!

We honored our humanity, regardless of differences.

Our focused, brush strokes on Life's canvas revealed our higher selves—

Attuned to GOD in all HIS forms and disguises, as people or events!

I am a replica of HIS caring nature when I care for the sick, weak, poor or aged,

And treat others the way I would like to be treated-

SHINE BRIGHT: INSIDE OUT, LIKE A CANDLE!

Rich or poor— upper class or lowest class,

We all need respect!

I am created to shine my flame of TRUTH in darkness!

CHAPTER 50 CANDLE

Time danced a tune, reverberating each person's contribution on Life's stage.

Return on investments?

Or

The proverbial wise and foolish virgins?

Karma? Payback for hurting others? Rewards?

Is there really "forgive and forget, without consequences?"

Is light the wisdom gleaned from your mistakes and mine?

Yes it means to do better in another set of similar circumstances – to show empathy or compassion, when needed.

One must choose wisdom over foolishness.

Wisdom gives me the right answers and foolishness sinks me in darkness-

Separation, poor choices and confusion.

Today, I choose to be wise to shine bright!

CHAPTER 51 QUESTIONS

A portrait of my bit of TRUTH, bought with struggles, tears,

Or siphoned information from seen or unseen Watchers-

Some guardians of TRUTH, others complete LIARS-preachers even.

Were Pharaoh's magicians any different from me?

Did I need Moses' serpentine powers to be a wise, biblical reptile?

Or a harmless, mammalian dove?

Is wisdom the key to my existence?

A Novice versus an illumined Master?

Is that like Jacob's rung ladder with angels ascending-?

Above and below?

Why the parables or Veil separating The Most Holy from The Holy in the Old Testament?

Who are the scoundrels outside your inner Kingdom?

Toxic people or institutions with ceremonial pomp– or laws of debauchery?

Do you believe a male was created to marry another male?

Yes or no? Freedom of choice, remember? And legal rights!

Secular or Spiritual effects? As above so below.

MASTER! You said in scripture,

"My sheep hear my voice!"

Am I a goat because I don't understand the Bible or Torah or Holy Koran?

MASTER my hearing is muffled by unexplained parables and

Misinterpretations of Holy Books and Mosques, Temples or Churches—help me!

Are there wisdom codes you hid to be deciphered-like Morse Codes for my complete illumination?

What of being labeled 'Illuminati" for asking seeker's questions?

"Seek and ye shall find"?

I heard you Lord, but I need more light!

CHAPTER 52 LIGHT?

Some iconic philanthropists were called out for being illumined- why?

Are some the proverbial stones GOD raised for Kingdom business now?

Because Original Blueprints-Heirs are brainwashed by idolized things or people or fear mongers and folk tales!

The GOOD BOOK said,

"The last shall be first, and the first last"

Others do good works yet some lobbyists fight to oppose the Good,

Some trample the laws of a GOD they once said they trusted,

Or

Is it the printed dollar sign their real God or the faces on those bills?

What happens if I destroy earth or people in the name of progress?

An exhaustive debate since Columbus sailed those three ships!

We argue medical innovations and trips to Mars – go explorers!

Were it not for innovators I would be writing with feathered pens or using only pencil and paper or pit toilets- no Bidets!

How much time before our actions eliminate the natural patterns of:

Birth, Life, Death and conservation of the earth?

I choose to be a harbinger of the WORK- all that is GOOD!

CHAPTER 53 ASSURANCE

Resurrection? Reincarnation?

I'm not sure of everything,

I bought insurance just in case.

I believe in the Resurrection:

Doubting Thomas convinced me!

I believe

I can't approach GOD as I am, without THE CHRIST:

The ONE who died on two crossed, tree branches between two thieves,

Pierced in HIS side, hands and feet!

The last Biblical, book implies:

Unbelievers and fearful people are collectively hopeless goats!

I am a sheep of the GOOD SHEPARD!

CHAPTER 54 EXAMPLES?

Why did Biblical Joseph have a cup of divination?

Was the cup one of MIND with a higher consciousness of GOD?

Or

Was that the mirror of his Choice?

How did Moses get those laws?

Forty days and nights, like Jesus' Temptation?

Why the cloud with the voice from Heaven after JESUS' Baptism?

Is that the same pillar of cloud that lead the Israelites out of Egypt?

Why all those metaphors, allegories and parables?

Argh! Speak plainly, I don't like **veiled** wordings!

Awakened me, is confused about **LIFE** and **DEATH**!

I clash with my main childhood profiler- Religion!

And others too – Philosophy, Psychology and Politics,

All in a match- single file,

Where are my teachers who made the introductions? Scram!

I see the Human Condition!

SHINE BRIGHT: INSIDE OUT, LIKE A CANDLE!

Why am I so messed up at times- a descendant of slaves- why?

Our uninformed are crushed by mass media with endless, mindless, reality scripted shows – while some Civil Rights are being stripped and Education being dumb down?

And where is my GOD in all of this?

HE speaks in Golden Silence, hidden in plain sight!

I must be informed to be a lighted, arrowed, flame!

R. Z. Joseph

CHAPTER 55 CLARITY

I internalized my life's experiences,

And gained my own interpretation of the Greatest Story ever told,

And, I surrendered to the GREAT I AM who reigns within!

Please answer these questions.

Why say the Other Power does not exist?

Didn't JESUS CHRIST confirm his existence when tempted by him for 40 days and 40 nights- Wasn't that Bright Star and one third of the angels kicked out of the Heavens -why?

Was there a political coup to overthrow a hierarchical order in the Heavens?

Was there a fake Manifesto used by the snake on Adam, Eve and us here on earth?

If Sin and Evil do not exist, then who created pedophiles and plane hijackers?

Why have security or put user identities on your devices?

Leave your Pandora locks, unlocked!

No secret signs, codes or handshakes!

And, why did CHRIST die to shed blood —HIS DNA matter, the unique portion that made him different?

To restore us to HIS Team after THE FALL?

R. Z. Joseph

To return spiritual clothes to our naked, uncovered flesh?

Or

To cover my exposed soul, the veiled, de fleshed, sacred parts?

Help me MASTER, I need more light to see!

CHAPTER 56 DEATH

And what of the sacrifices of those disciples, JESUS' followers?

10 of them with the exception of John the Revelator, died cruel deaths-

On different, shaped crosses:

Peter who forsook him thrice and repented, chose an X shaped cross,

Because he did not feel worthy to die on a crossed tree, like JESUS CHRIST.

Why were the disciples crucified if the Bible is a book of fables and allegories?

And JESUS was a Way Shower, but not THE WAY?

Is there a new propaganda of a first coming of another Master?

Is this the anticipated False Christ with a false prophet?

An attempt to fortify the false beliefs of foolish, goats?

Do they look for signs in contrived, unlit, dark candles?

What of lit Martyrs like Joan of Arc, Martin Luther King and Garvey?

All killed for freeing us from shadows in our mirrors?

What forces influenced those killings- if not GOOD, then what's the opposite?

Who or what spill their blood and why?

Can you tell me without any double talk or lie?

Is death an illusion?

Why did JESUS raise Lazarus after four days – to die a second physical death to be resurrected? Whoa!

Why can't I resolve my inner questionings if JESUS IS THE ANSWER?

CHAPTER 57 DARKNESS

Who is the God of Forces mentioned in the Old Testament?

What is HIS role?

Church folks, get out of my way!

Do not quench my soul's hunger for

The Fruit of Wisdom to sprint to the Tree of Life!

I am tired of seeking hidden, manna in phantom minds,

And those who sing their platitudes,

As I sink in miry clay of flesh!

All phantoms do, is leave behind a broken trail to nowhere-

And more questions, without answers!

Why taunt sincere, seekers?

Is this part of the arduous process?

The more I seek to know,

Other hard questions unfurl to hurl me in a whirl,

Back to zero, in a dark, brooding search- why?

Would my power centers- Chakras, well endowed- declare the TRUTH to set me free?

Top, Crown Chakra – well veiled by practicing believers.

I surrender all-

I know there is no escaping of

I AM THAT I AM within- I am of I AM, really?

CHAPTER 58 MIRROR

As new awareness came,

A self-consciousness arose.

My intuitive eyes scanned--

Beyond the boundaries of soul.

Spirit-Mind left Kingdom,

Perception of shadows for reality:

Strife, fears, idolatry, foolish desires,

And the list goes on.

My eyes darted from fellow artists to detractors—

A weak moment.

I lost touch with my naked genius on life's canvas.

And felt myself slip out of my inner, sacred space-

That knew no limitations.

I had forgotten the TRUTH of my existence:

Born a winner, an overcomer,

With seeming, miraculous abilities

SHINE BRIGHT: INSIDE OUT, LIKE A CANDLE!

Attuned to GOD THE I AM
Everything is possible to me!
I can shine as bright as the haloed sun!

CHAPTER 59 FAIL, THEN SUCCEED!

I was back where I'd started- fleshed!
Fully clothed in earthly regalia,
To examine my human weaknesses-
Without judging yours.
I shouted, angrily to no one in particular:
"Forget you all"
Thou shall not cuss? I did not curse!

My mood went from one of euphoric bliss,
To a low tone of artistic despair,
When writer's block becomes a staple food—my daily fare,
And the delete key seem a suitable choice!

I could not go back to my pure,
And unashamed state as a Creative being,
I needed help to return to purity of purpose,
Before I got distracted by weights- my shadows included.
Failure is not an option!
Let there be light- and the Golden Silence was broken!

CHAPTER 60 SUCCESS

A major lesson learned:
A disciplined mind will produce
The resilience of an Army Marshall,
To conquer any mood swing which tries to derail
A precise war strategy in the army of THE KING!
A war of self, created by shadows,
As the Holy Spirit tries to reconnect me
Back to GOD,
The ONE TRUE, LIFE SOURCE.

As I picked up the faces and names I'd tossed aside,
I remembered a great law:
UNIVERSAL TRUTH always
Reward right intentions, thoughts and actions.
And conscious world Servers are destined to contribute,
To all that is good and just,
Regardless of our different cultures, world views or beliefs.
I am a conscious Server of Goodwill!

R. Z. Joseph

CHAPTER 61 HERE TO SERVE

We are here to play our individual tunes,

Despite our philosophical views or questions.

Who else can cure our ills?

We're God's hands with our little wills,

To be HIS uncovered lights,

To follow wherever HE leads based on our skills sets—like:

Mandela of South Africa who resisted Apartheid,

Gandhi of India who resisted national servitude to Colonialism,

King of America who fought for Civil Rights for Blacks,

Mother Theresa who rescued the poor from rat, infested garbage in India,

And the list continues with you and me.

Peace lovers are tired of child soldiers in Darfur,

Hitler-like characters anywhere on our globe must be stopped!

We will shine bright with the right information and training,

To eradicate conflicts for nuclear weaponry or destruction,

A new day has come to Shine Bright Inside Out like a Candle!

R. Z. Joseph

CHAPTER 62 THE CALL

Our Global Village has two types of individuals—

One group knows global, planetary life has an expiry date-

To do right and enjoy our God given benefits as Children of God.

And others who misuse time and resources to destroy people and planet for profit.

How much wealth is enough for you to live in gluttony?

Remember the French Guillotine for greedy goats?

Thank God, Retribution for wrongs is the great equalizer, not violence.

I hear CHRIST say to the wise,

"Welcome to those who heard the same tunes,

Beyond the audible ears and did my WILL for the Kingdom!"

In amazement, I exclaimed,

"I know that voice!

I have to remove those clothes, veil or flesh, both must scram!

I have to go within the Kingdom, again- fast!

Get out of my way- toxic people and situations-

Good days start again today,

I am of I AM is here to stay!

Shine Bright: Inside Out, like a Candle!

"See y'all later!"

SHINE BRIGHT: INSIDE OUT, LIKE A CANDLE!

R. Z. Joseph

About the Author

A passionate advocate for Self-Improvement and Literacy.

Joseph has a Bachelor of Arts Degree in Social Studies and currently pursuing further studies.

A New Yorker, Joseph is very patriotic to the ideals of Democracy for which the United States of America is the greatest Global Star.

A former Public Servant/Educator with several years of teaching and managing employment training programs in the West Indies.

R.Z. Joseph is a Motivational Coach and Author.

Founder and Managing Director of New Dreams, Colors and Faces, an American Small Business that promotes literature on Self-Reliance and Self-Esteem in the Global Economy.

Hobbies: reading, making candles, painting, writing and traveling.

Sale of this book contribute to an outreach program for immigrants

© 2013 ALL RIGHTS RESERVED. ALL CANDLES AND 2 PAINTINGS ARE THE CREATION OF R.Z. JOSEPH AND CANNOT BE COPIED, SOLD OR USED WITHOUT PERMISSION.

5 Rights I Value Most

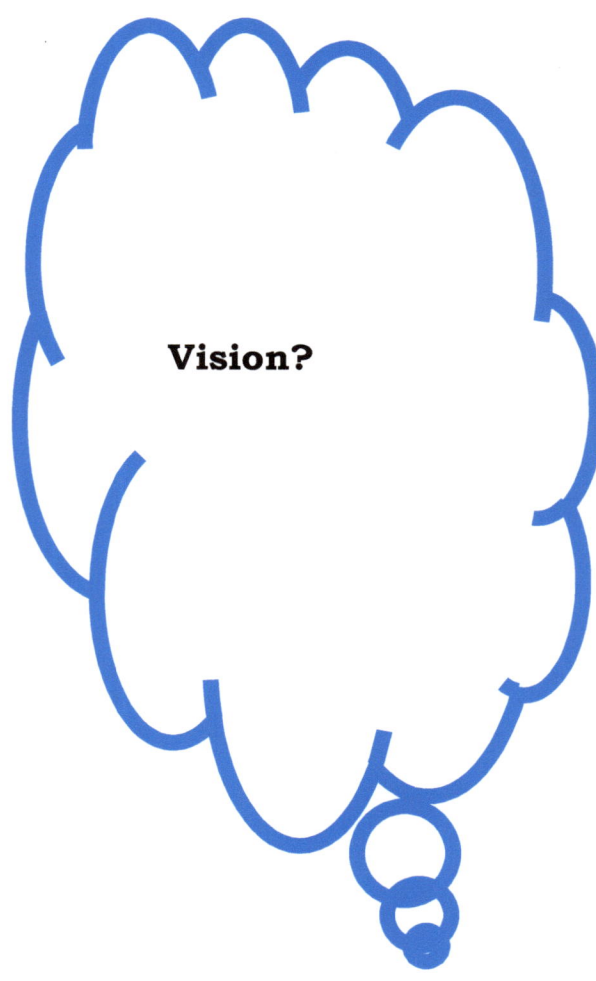

SHINE BRIGHT: INSIDE OUT, LIKE A CANDLE!

2 MAJOR GOALS WITHIN 1 Yr.

R. Z. Joseph

3 Things I Agree or Disagree With

WISDOM CODES:
1. Stay away from negative vibes.
2. Think for myself.
3. Love myself……..
4. Treat others well.

R. Z. Joseph

COURTESIES

Original King James Bible

Rights of Man, Thomas Paine 1774-1779.

National Human Genome Research Institute, USA.

(Public Domain/Fair Use)

This book is the original, artistic interpretation of the author.

COPYRIGHT 2013. ALL RIGHTS RESERVED.

Self-Awareness

1. Life –long learning.
2. Good health.
3. Social Environment: family/home, friends, school, clubs etc.
4. Religion or Spirituality.
5. Nutritious food
6.

R. Z. Joseph

www.ingramcontent.com/pod-product-compliance
Lightning Source LLC
Chambersburg PA
CBHW042303150426
43196CB00005B/61